Virtual
Team
Building
Exercises

Virtual Team Building Exercises

A Guide to Managing Human Resources over Space and Time

by

Robert Andrejev

DORRANCE PUBLISHING CO., INC.
PITTSBURGH, PENNSYLVANIA 15222

For information or to order additional books, please write:
Dorrance Publishing Co., Inc.
701 Smithfield Street
Third Floor
Pittsburgh, Pennsylvania 15222
U.S.A.
1-800-788-7654
Or visit our website and online catalogue at www.dorrancebookstore.com

I would like to dedicate this book to
my family and friends,
who have inspired me to become a better man
and a more confident person.

Contents

Introduction

According to the 2005 copy of the Webster's II New College Dictionary, Third Edition,[1] the word **virtual** is defined as "existing or resulting in effect or essence though not in actual fact, form, or name." The word **team** is defined as "a group organized to work together." Today's organizations span across floors, buildings, lands, and seas. From personal experience, I have worked in a variety of organizations and groups that crossed each of these areas. Creativity in the workplace is most important when trying to build a cohesive group. When working together on tasks or projects, success will increase if everyone gets along. In recent years, more and more organizations have been expanding to include team members from other organizations and from other locations. With a group of people located around the world, previous types of team building exercises do not have the same impact and outcomes. Thus, Virtual Team Building Exercises need to come into play to build cohesive groups.

A variety of simple exercises can be built from any one idea. In the following chapters, you will read about using those skills and creative ideas that are common to all human beings. Also, this book has been written to bring out the creativity of any one team member or group of team members, so that they can express their creative sides and assist groups to bond and be as

---

[1] Copyright © 2005 by Houghton Mifflin Company. Adapted and reproduced by permission from Webster's II New College Dictionary, Third Edition.

successful as they can be. We are all children at heart, so we need to hold on to that part of us, which is evident throughout our adult lives.

As groups grow and become more global, the leader should begin by getting the team members involved. Below is a simple structure that can be used to induce creativity and team building concepts or ideas:

- Locations
- Request Suggestions
- Categorize Ideas
- Document/Present/Complete

Locations

There are a variety of ways that a leader can gather information about his or her team members. One way is to request the information directly from the team members. Questionnaires or surveys can be completed so that the leader can understand what locations they can focus on to build exercises. Research of these areas and of the local events, weather, and points of interest can be gathered and used. By requesting such information directly from the team members, it allows for their involvement and sharing of information. The anticipation can be very intriguing to anyone.

Request Suggestions

Not only should you gather your own information, but you can also consolidate ideas and suggestions from the team members themselves. Many people have ideas, but they may not have an outlet. Opening the door for someone to share his or her ideas can increase the success of any team.

Categorize Ideas

After capturing information, ideas, and suggestions, you will want to create a database of sorts. By keeping all the gathered information in one manageable location, you can easily access any specific details, and by analyzing the different pieces of data, you may come up with other ideas altogether.

Document/Present/Complete

The leader can choose one or two ideas (from the team members or from him or her) to begin the team building exercises. Depending on the frequency of team meetings, you may want to choose a variety of ideas or a stream of ideas that have a connection between one another. Some situations allow for team meetings to be held weekly, monthly, quarterly. Following a monthly team meeting regime, you can plan up to twelve exercises, which can be prepared and used to motivate attendance of the meetings. Keeping everyone interested is not only the leader's responsibility, but it is also the responsibility of the team members themselves. Commitment to the group by everyone should be expressed at every meeting. Knowing that some may or may not be available, the leader must make every effort to not cancel any team meeting (schedule other meetings around the established team meeting). This demonstrates that the leader is leading by example.

Being creative in ways to motivate team members can be done in various ways. The following chapters will share with you examples that have been created creatively.

Chapter 1 — Five Senses

Depending on the people within the group, the leader should verify if any or all of the five senses can be common across the team. No matter where they are located, the leader can use current communication tools (e.g., e-mail, hardcopy mail, phones, conference phones, Internet connectivity, face-to-face conversations, meetings, etc.). The following are examples, based on the five human senses, which can be used to build team cohesiveness and stimulate creative ideas.

Should any one of the team members bring new ideas to the leader, the ideas should be given serious consideration. The ideas can be detailed by the team member and saved into a specific file for future consideration or implementation.

The following examples can allow leaders to stimulate new ideas for the same five senses, which are common between all team members and organizations.

Sense–Seeing

Here is a seeing-related team building exercise:

- Set up a team meeting and make sure you have the appropriate connections for everyone that are not at the leader's location. (See earlier listing of some communication tools that are available today.)
- Ask everyone to have a blank piece of paper and a pencil.
- The directions are given through the communication tool being used, and each person must write down what he or she thinks is being described.
- Time constraints can be implemented by the leader, but the leader must take into consideration how much time is feasible for the various team members to understand and complete the exercise.
- Communicate the questions so the team members can write down their answers. See next page for examples.

The leader can create a committee that will review and select those with the most correct answers.

- Winner(s) will be announced at the next team meeting (motivation to attend).
- Prizes can be sent out to those who had the most correct. (Prizes: Items can be as simple as an item for the work desk.)
- The leader can use a teaser and announce the next sense for the next team meeting. (Senses can be repeated depending on the success of each one tried.)

Note: *Motivation comes in all forms. Inexpensive items can be enough because the team members are being acknowledged. Past experience proves that the prizes do not have to be expensive.*

Questions	Possible Answers
English (and/or other cultural languages' words containing the letter combinations ii or uu or aa or ww or vv are rare. Can you think of one of each?	Skiing; Taxiing; Radii, Vacuum; Continuum, Bazaar, Powwow, Savvy; Flivver
What is being described in this riddle? When I am filled, I can point the way. When I am empty, Nothing moves me.	A glove
Anagrams: For each of the following expressions, rearrange the letters to make another expression. Do not add or subtract any letters. (Hint: #1. is a two-word phrase; #2. is a three-word phrase.) No City Dust Here does ease thirst STRATEGY: Guess and check with each letter written on a small piece of paper.	1. The countryside 2. The Desert Oasis

Sense–Hearing

Here is a hearing related team building exercise:
- Set up a team meeting and make sure you have the appropriate connections for everyone that are not at the leader's location. (see earlier listing of some communication tools that are available today)
- Ask everyone to have a blank piece of paper and a pencil.
- The directions are given through the communication tool being used and each person must write down what he or she thinks is being heard.
- Communicate the questions so the team members can write down their answers. Here are some examples:

Sound Makers
- Using a cup of water, held at an angle, allow water to drip out onto a metal plate of sorts
- Using two pencils, make drumming sounds on a desk
- Tap keys on keyboard
- Run finger along the lip of a glass of water in a fast motion to cause a whistling effect
- Use a stapler to staple sheets of paper
- Bounce a stress ball on the desktop until it vibrates to a stop
- Remove and replace a cap on a marker multiple times

The leader can create a committee that will review and select those with the most correct answers.

- Winner(s) will be announced at the next team meeting (motivation to attend).
- Prizes can be sent out to those who had the most correct. (Prizes: Items can be as simple as an item for the work desk.)

- The leader can use a teaser and announce the next sense for the next team meeting (Senses can be repeated depending on the success of each one tried.)

Note: *Since the teams can be made up of all kinds of team members, you may have a hearing impaired team member, who can show he or she is able to do what the others can with the appropriate tools. This helps others with no experience, to have a positive one. This also increases the success of the team during projects by just being cohesive.*

Sense–Smelling

Here is a smelling related team building exercise:

- Set up a team meeting, and make sure you have the appropriate connections for everyone that are not at the leader's location. (See earlier listing of some communication tools that are available today.)
- Ask that one piece of paper captures all of the responses and the team member's name.
- The directions are given through the communication tool being used and each person must write down what he or she thinks is being smelled. (Team members will try to determine the smell of substances with blindfolds over their eyes.)

Note: *The leader will need to prepare packages of bandanas and numbered items in containers, or a listing of items for a focal point at each site to prepare. The focal point can be a team member or another leader who is willing to participate as the on-site leader.*

- Communicate by stating the numbered items in order. The team members can state their answers, while the focal point lists the responses down on the paper. Here are some examples:

- ○ Raw onion
- ○ Slice of potato
- ○ Chocolate
- ○ Lemon powder
- ○ Dirt
- ○ Shampoo
- ○ Pencil shavings
- ○ Toothpaste
- ○ Paper
- ○ Ink
- ○ Sugar

- Ask the team members if they are confident that they could determine what items they smell without seeing the items.
- Tell the team members that they are going to perform a test to find out if their predictions were correct
- Have the team members break into two groups at each site. Each team member plugs his or her nose while blindfolded and smell various substances.
- Once they have smelled the substances, the team members are instructed to try to identify each substance, and the focal point leader writes down their responses on the piece of paper. If they just cannot distinguish what the scent is, they can write down that they do not know. As each team member takes the test, check off, on his or her list which substances are correctly identified, which are incorrectly identified, and which responses are "I don't know."

The leader can create a committee that will review and select those with the most correct answers.

- Winner(s) will be announced at the next team meeting (motivation to attend).

- Prizes can be sent out to those who had the most correct. (Prizes: items can be as simple as an item for the work desk.)
- The leader can use a teaser and announce the next sense for the next team meeting (Senses can be repeated depending on the success of each one tried.)
- Encourage team members to take this same test with their families or friends to do further research and to bring home some of the lighter side of working for a living.

Sense—Tasting

Here is a **tasting** related team building exercise:

- Set up a team meeting and make sure you have the appropriate connections for everyone that are not at the leader's location. (See earlier listing of some communication tools that are available today.)
- Ask that one piece of paper captures all of the guesses and a team member's name.
- The directions are given through the communication tool being used and each person must write down what he or she thinks is being smelled (Team members will try to determine the flavor of substances with blindfolds over their eyes)

Note: *The leader will need to prepare packages of gourmet jelly beans and a color combination chart to provide to a focal point at each site. The focal point can also be asked to prepare the packages for his or her particular site. The focal point can be a team member or another leader who is willing to participate as the on-site leader.*

- Combinations of gourmet jelly beans (by colors) are selected so that each site has the same color combinations.

- Using the communication tool for the meeting, the predetermined combinations of colors are announced. Each team member tastes them and writes down what he or she tastes.
- Once the combinations are tried, each team member sends his or her list of answers to the leader.

The leader can create a committee that will review and select those with the most correct answers.

- Winner(s) will be announced at the next team meeting (motivation to attend).
- Prizes can be sent out to those who had the most correct. (Prizes: Items can be as simple as an item for the work desk.)
- The leader can use a teaser and announce the next sense for the next team meeting. (Senses can be repeated depending on the success of each one tried.)
- Encourage team members to take this same test with their families or friends to do further research and to bring home some of the lighter side of working for a living.

Sense–Touching

Here is a **touching** related team building exercise:

- Set up a team meeting and make sure you have the appropriate connections for everyone that are not at the leader's location. (See earlier listing of some communication tools that are available today.)
- Ask that one piece of paper captures all of the responses and a team member's name.
- The directions are given through the communication tool being used and each person must write down what he or she thinks is being touched. (Team members will try to

determine substances by touch with blindfolds over their eyes.)

Note: *The leader will need to prepare packages of bandanas and numbered items in containers, or a listing of items for a focal point at each site to prepare. The focal point can be a team member or another leader who is willing to participate as the on-site leader.*

Items to touch

- ° Damp cloth
- ° Eraser with chalk powder
- ° Chilled pen
- ° Sticks of gum
- ° Popcorn (older, so the smell does not give it away)
- ° Glob of glue on the tip of a marker
- ° Chilled paper punch

The leader can create a committee that will review and select those with the most correct answers.

- Winner(s) will be announced at the next team meeting (motivation to attend).
- Prizes can be sent out to those who had the most correct (Prizes: Items can be as simple as an item for the work desk.)
- The leader can use a teaser and announce the next sense for the next team meeting (Senses can be repeated depending on the success of each one tried.)

Chapter 2 — Baby Picture Match Up

Everyone was a child once; the Baby Picture Match-Up is a great team building exercise, which can be accomplished as a virtual team building exercise. It is a fun way to get people to know each other by face and by name. Having the contest as a web-based game makes it accessible around the world. Even though not everyone will work together face-to-face, they may work together over the phone, through a video conference, or in any number of ways. Familiarity with your team members could influence your projects' outcomes in certain aspects.

Pre-Work

The leader can prepare pre-work for this team building exercise:

- Request two photos of each member, a baby photo and an adult photo
- Set up a webpage to host the photos (if available)
- Set up start and end dates for team member entries
- The photos "due by" date should allow time to upload to the website
- Once the photos have been received, the photos should be numbered, and the matched numbers should be kept in a secured area, so that the leader can build up even more excitement
- Promotional announcements can build up to this team building exercise

Playing the Virtual Team Building Exercise

- Team members submit their responses, between start and end dates, to the leader.
- The leader can date and time stamp the entries, so that the submissions of the team members are placed in order of receipt.

Post-Work

Once the team building exercise has been completed, the next steps can be the following:

- The leader will review and select those with the most correct answers in the order received
- Winner(s) will be announced at the next team meeting (motivation to attend).
- Prizes can be sent out to those who had the most correct. (Prizes: Items can be as simple as an item for the work desk.)
- The leader can use a teaser and announce the next **"Virtual Team Building Exercise"** for the next team meeting. (Exercises can be repeated depending on the success of each one tried.)

The leader can use this as a tool to increase team member awareness. Also, funny photos are most interesting. Having these photos as story starters at the team meeting can allow for increased awareness between team members. This type of team building also allows team members to share some of their experiences about themselves, their accomplishments, their families or whatever pops up! Culture sharing in this manner may be the only exposure some team members may have in their lifetimes. (Can you see how one team building exercise can jump start future team building exercises?)

Another point to be made is that not every organization has access to web-pages or websites. Not a problem—just create electronic photo boards of the photos, one grouping of baby photos and one board with adult photos. This could be sent electronically or printed and sent out in hard copy form. Another opportunity for creativity—how can your group make this a success?

Chapter 3 — Who's Who

Remembering the various age groups that make up today's workforce, a leader needs to keep this in mind when planning team building exercises. So many shows are coming back from the past, to which the younger generation can now relate. Blending the shows from yesterday and the technology of today can bring everyone together. Web-based exercises will allow more team members to interact in a real-time mind-set. Television game shows were very popular in their day. To begin, two teams can be created over a conference call or video conference, depending on the locations of team members. Here are some steps to follow for the leader and the team members:

Pre-Work
- Request a secret or interesting fact from each team member, about themselves.
- Create a panel of three team members.
- The panel has to answer as if each had the secret.

Playing the Virtual Team Building Exercise
- Each team asks anyone on the panel three questions.
- Teams discuss and venture their guess as to who is telling the truth.
- Guesses are made.
- The actual person announces who owns the secret!

Post-Work

- Prizes can be given out to those who had the correct guess (Prizes: Items can be as simple as an item for the work desk).
- The leader can use a teaser and announce the next **Virtual Team Building Exercise** for the next team meeting. (Exercises can be repeated depending on the success of each one tried.)

Chapter 4 — Draw to Win

As you try to find new ideas that will include everyone and motivate them to get involved, you may fall back on some team building exercises that we use to do as children. Drawing has always been a child's favorite way of expressing him or herself. Good or bad, children try their best. Parents will hang up anything and everything that their children create. The same holds true for adults at family get-togethers or even just a group of friends hanging out for an evening of fun. Drawing and playing "guess what this is" has been part of game playing for many years. The following is a derivation of an old theme:

Pre-Work
- The leader creates a list of items to draw.
- The leader divides up the team members into groups.

Playing the Virtual Team Building Exercise
- The first team member selected has one minute to draw using an electronic drawing board.
- The rest of the team has one minute to guess and win a point.
- The second team has a chance to venture a guess, if the first team does not successfully guess what has been drawn and win a point.
- If the guesses are incorrect, the team member announces what he or she was drawing, and no one wins a point.

- The first team to ten points (or whatever the leader decides) wins the game.

Post-Work

- Prizes can be given out to the team that had the most correct guesses. (Prizes: Items can be as simple as an item for the work desk.)
- The leader can use a teaser and announce the next Virtual Team Building Exercise for the next team meeting.

Chapter 5 — Card Games

Card games are vast around the world. Various cultures have their own card games that they play. In Italy, a game is called Scopa. In the United States, a game is called Euchre. This Virtual Team Building Exercise can only be done with the most creative leaders and/or team members.

One type of card game that can be played uses Internet websites that allow private rooms for playing with team members. The leader can set up a private room and grant access to team members as the meeting begins. Various card games are available.

The leader should also determine which games will be played. If the team members are from various parts of the world, the leader can send out directions and how-to-play instructions, so the team members will be familiar before the virtual team building exercise commences.

Pre-Work

- The leader should review where the team members are located and what types of card games are played in those regions.
- The leader may also ask the team what they would like to play and choose based on a consensus of the team.
- Depending on what type of card game the leader decides to play, the team should begin practicing or sharing how to play with other team members, for those who are less experienced.

Playing the Virtual Team Building Exercise

- Once the team meeting begins, the leader decides when to start play.
- The leader selects the first item and announces it to the team, the website address, and any access codes needed to enter the room.
- Team members begin playing.
- The game continues until someone completes a round or whenever the leader decides to end the game.
- The leader verifies the game winner.

Post-Work

- Prizes can be given out to the team member(s) who had won. (Prizes: Items can be as simple as an item for the work desk.)
- The leader can use a teaser and announce the next Virtual Team Building Exercise for the next team meeting.

Chapter 6 — Origami Game

The act of listening to directions and applying what is heard or learned is another very useful tool in the success of projects. Clients may ask you to produce something they want. You, as a support person, must understand what they want before you can produce anything. Team members are human; thus issues with communication may always creep up. Taking the time to listen is as important as knowing how to produce a product or service.

Keeping this in mind, the art of origami is to understand directions (sometimes with diagrams and sometimes without). This type of exercise can help team members increase their listening and direction following skills. Below is a fun team building exercise:

Pre-Work
The leader can prepare pre-work for this team building exercise:

- The Leader can gather a variety of origami examples from the public library, the Internet, and other sources.

Playing the Virtual Team Building Exercise
- During the team meeting, the leader reads the step-by-step directions and allows approximately one minute for each step.
- Once the directions are communicated to the team, each team member has five minutes to finish creating their origami product.

Example: *This box made from two bills. The bills/box can be the gift itself, but it is also just about the right size to be a ring box.*

- Get yourself two fairly new, crisp bills. For this design to work, the folds should be very precise, perpendicular to the edges of the bill if the result is to be rectangular.
- Lay the bill face up on a flat surface. Fold the bill in thirds lengthwise, as shown. Gently unfold these folds; you will reuse them later. I will refer to these as the third folds
- Fold the bill from top to bottom just to the right of the portrait; then unfold. Repeat just to the left of the portrait. I will refer to these as the portrait folds. Note that the third folds oppose (are perpendicular to) the portrait folds.
- Starting at the top left corner, close the top third fold to about ninety degrees. Lift the right edge of the bill to the right of the right portrait fold while holding the top third fold in place, allowing the third fold to close completely to the right of this corner.
- Inside this corner will be a remaining portion that you will crease along the natural forty-five degree line to complete the corner.
- Complete the previous step for the other three corners. Now you will have two "tabs" sticking up on the left and right sides.
- For each tab, pull it inside the box, folding so that the natural edge of the box is pulled slightly over inside the fold.
- Do this evenly for both tabs.
- For the two other sides, evenly fold over the edge of the bill.
- You should now have an open box.
- If you make another piece just like the first, but slightly larger, you will have a lid similar to that found on most

shoe boxes. To adjust the instructions above, fold so
that the inner rectangle (bounded by the third and portrait folds) is slightly larger

- Fold the second bill lengthwise so that the width matches the widest portion of the open box you just made. I
will refer to this bill as the cover and the previous piece
made as the open box in the following steps.

- You need two folds as shown to be able to follow the last
step. For general appearance, it is nice if these are near-
ly symmetrical, as shown. These will be called the width
folds.

- Holding one end of the cover across the bottom of the
open box, find the point which matches the corner of
the open box, and fold at that point.

- After folding, open the fold to ninety degrees, hold the
cover back in place, and find the point for the next corner of the open box as the cover wraps around.

- Repeat this process until the cover wraps over itself (four
folds).These will be called the wrapping folds

- There is now one very long side to the cover. Fold back
the long side so that is just a bit shorter than the first
side. I will call this the end cover fold

- The end cover fold is at the left edge. I have also completely unfolded the cover, refolded the end cover fold,
the width folds, then the wrapping folds in that order.
(This unfolding/refolding is optional.)

- In either case, the end cover fold puts the remainder
from the long side inside the wrapping folds. Refold the
wrapping folds, holding the long side in place to crease
it at the correct points.

- Open up the width folds slightly on the open end, and
insert the last side under the width folds.

- Slide the open box inside the cover before closing the

cover tightly, or close the cover with the open box already inside. In either case, you are done

Post-Work

Once the team building exercise has been completed, the next steps can be the following:

- The leader requests all team members to submit their final products for review.
- Winner(s) will be announced at the next team meeting (motivation to attend).
- Prizes can be sent out to those who had the best end product based on the directions given. (Prizes: Items can be as simple as an item for the work desk.)
- The leader can use a teaser and announce the next Virtual Team Building Exercise for the next team meeting.

Chapter 7 — Scavenger Hunt

During the changing seasons, weather changes and nights begin to last longer. This is a perfect time of year for a scavenger hunt. Being aware of various cultures, team members can play the same game around their office environments. This can be played during a team meeting, and it can motivate everyone through activity. Below is a fun team building exercise:

Pre-Work

The leader can prepare pre-work for this team building exercise:

- The leader can create a list of items that can be typically found in an office environment.
- The list can be ready to present at the team meeting with a predetermined time frame for the hunt.

Playing the Virtual Team Building Exercise

- The leader can announce the hunt will begin once the listing of items has been communicated to all the team members at the same time.
- The timeframe can be started (fifteen minutes) once the items have been communicated
- Example of items to be scavenged:
    - Black stapler
    - Picture in a frame with at least two people
    - Picture of an animal

- ° Company logo
- ° Coffee mug
- ° Six paper clips
- ° Paper towel roll

Post-Work

Once the team building exercise has completed, the next steps can be the following:

- The leader requests all team members to announce once they have retrieved all the items within the allotted time frame.
- Winner(s) will be announced at the next team meeting (motivation to attend).
- Prizes can be sent out to those who completed the hunt in the shortest time frame. (Prizes: Items can be as simple as an item for the work desk.)
- The leader can use a teaser and announce the next Virtual Team Building Exercise for the next team meeting.

Chapter 8 — Mind Bogglers

Having the variety of skills, education, and experiences, team members bring a plethora of knowledge. Using your brain is just as important as using your brawn in many situations. To test the mind and get everyone involved, the following are some mind boggling brain teasers that can be created by thinking about what type of challenge the leader wants to put in front of the team. Below is a fun team building exercise:

Pre-Work
- The leader can research what mind boggler(s) are to be used.
- Topics can vary from work, to geographic locations, or any other area of interest.
- The time frame can be started once the mind boggler(s) are communicated.
- The ending time can be what the leader determines is feasible for the various locations where the team members reside.

Playing the Virtual Team Building Exercise
- The leader can communicate each mind boggler.
- The following are examples:

Using three to four consecutive letters from any word as the clue, determine a word that contains these letters: y p s

Hypsography
Hypsometer
Hypsometry

Using three to four consecutive letters from any word as the clue, determine a word that contains these letters: y l b u
> Phenylbutazone

Using three to four consecutive letters from any word as the clue, determine a word that contains these letters: a c e u
> Pharmaceutical

Using three to four consecutive letters from any word as the clue, determine word that contains these letters: u s s a
> Decussate

Using three to four consecutive letters from any word as the clue, determine a word that contains these letters: e b r
> Hebrew

Using three to four consecutive letters from any word as the clue, determine a word that contains these letters: i r i g
> Kirigami

Using three to four consecutive letters from any word as the clue, determine a word that contains these letters: e u t e
> Lieutenant

Using three to four consecutive letters from any word as the clue, determine a word that contains these letters: a i e u
> Maieutic

Using three to four consecutive letters from any word as the clue, determine a word that contains these letters: e i o

    Meiotic

    Meiosis

Using three to four consecutive letters from any word as the clue, determine a word that contains these letters: i d g i

    Pidgin

Using three to four consecutive letters from any word as the clue, determine a word that contains these letters: c t u

    Picture

Using three to four consecutive letters from any word as the clue, determine a word that contains these letters: n i t u

    Plenitude

Using three to four consecutive letters from any word as the clue, determine a word that contains these letters: a l i f

    Qualify

    Qualified

Using three to four consecutive letters from any word as the clue, determine a word that contains these letters: b s c

    Subscribe

Using three to four consecutive letters from any word as the clue, determine a word that contains these letters: u r c

    Resource

    Resources

Using three to four consecutive letters from any word as the clue, determine a word that contains these letters: e s s i

Professional

Blessing

Using three to four consecutive letters from any word as the clue, determine a word that contains these letters: v i v i

Vivisection

Using three to four consecutive letters from any word as the clue, determine a word that contains these letters: s c l

Disclosure

Disclosures

Using three to four consecutive letters from any word as the clue, determine a word that contains these letters: a t t o

Tattoo

Using three to four consecutive letters from any word as the clue, determine a word that contains these letters: e e t l

Beetle

Post-Work

Once the team building exercise has been completed, the next steps can be the following:

- The leader requests that all team members send their answer(s) through an electronic medium after a predetermined timeframe—the first with all the correct answer(s) or the member with the most correct answer(s) wins the prize.
- Winner will be announced at the next team meeting (motivation to attend).
- The prize can be sent out to the winner(s) (Prizes: Items can be as simple as an item for the work desk.)

- The leader can use a teaser and announce the next Virtual Team Building Exercise for the next team meeting.

Chapter 9 — Team Member Bingo

Bingo is a game that has been played by all ages, school children through senior citizens. This game has been played in many derivations. Thus, the leader can create his or her version. Using the diverse cultures that make up the team, or anything that is known across the group, is a good idea (e.g. It can be as simple as color matching or as challenging as major tourist attractions in various countries). Should anyone have input, team members can help create the boards for the bingo game. Their involvement should increase the cohesiveness of the group, through simple interaction amongst the team members. Below is a fun team building exercise:

Pre-Work
- The leader can either request team member participation to create the boards or use the information about the various team members to create the boards.
- Each square can contain an interesting fact about team members or numbers.
- Items to cover those squares that are called out can be hard chips, which can be keepsakes, or an office marker that can mark the squares.
- Electronic boards can be created and shared using conference capabilities (e.g. video conferencing).
- The leader should plan on having a variety of prizes for a variety of winning patterns (e.g. diagonal line, straight line, top-down/bottom-up, four corners, etc.).

Playing the Virtual Team Building Exercise

- The time frame can be started once the game rules have been communicated.
- The ending time can be what the leader determines is feasible for the various types of wins within one game or multiple games.
- The leader chooses the way the items will be selected and called out over the predetermined communication tool (e.g. a shared screen can list the items called out; the leader can pull items out of a bag; etc.)
- Team members are encouraged to be the first to call out once they meet the winning layout.
- Ties can be determined by the leader, or both can win a prize once the winning lines are verified.

Post-Work

Once the team building exercise has been completed, the next steps can be the following:

- The prizes can be sent out to the winning team members. (Prizes: Items can be as simple as an item for the work desk.)
- The leader can use a teaser and announce the next Virtual Team Building Exercise for the next team meeting.

Chapter 10 — Recipe Contest

Recipe contests have been held for many occasions and for charities. In this case, a leader can motivate those team members who enjoy cooking or baking, while motivating others to be judges. This type of exercise can help team members increase their interactions with one another, as well as enhance group participation, since not everyone may want to enter the contest. Here is what is suggested:

Note: *This Virtual Team Building Exercise is rather tricky, since the entrees must be tasted by the judges. This may not work for all organizations or groups, but it is worth the time to try and figure out if it would work for your group.*

Pre-Work
- The leader can present the idea to see how many would like to participate.
- After determining the categories that will be allowed, the leader can request those team members to submit their recipes by a certain date.
- Once the date is set and the recipes have been entered, the leader can plan a get-together (at a local park, conference room, or other selected location).

Playing the Virtual Team Building Exercise

- The team members bring their entries to the predetermined location.
- The judges also arrive at the predetermined location.
- The leader begins the exercise by allowing the judges to sample all of the entries.
- After all entries have been sampled, the judges take some time to confer and determine the first, second, and third place winners.
- The leader announces the winners, and prizes are handed out.

Post-Work

Once the team building exercise has been completed, the next steps can be the following:

- The leader requests that all team members enjoy all of the entries.
- The leader can use a teaser and announce the next Virtual Team Building Exercise for the next team meeting.

Chapter 11 — Figure-It-Out Game

Challenges come in various forms. Every day we have situations that make us stop and think. This game is just another one of those weird types of situations. Using our minds to answer questions, resolve issues, or just communicate with others will be enhanced by playing the Figure-It-Out game. Below is another challenging Virtual Team Building Exercise:

Pre-Work
- The leader can research what types of challenges will be presented.
- Using the Internet, other leaders, or just examples below will do the trick.
- Have all the challenges ready for the team members to figure out (either individually or together).

Playing the Virtual Team Building Exercise
- The time frame can be started once the items have been communicated.
- Some examples of what challenges can be addressed are below:

Figure It Out
Unscramble the following to make "ONLY ONE WORD"
yorndoolwen
Answer: ONLY ONE WORD
Unscramble the following: *coeuserr*

Answer: Resource

Riddle: What is white in the air and yellow on the ground?
Answer: An Egg

What is a *pannikin*?
Answer: A small saucepan or metal cup

What is *pteridology*?
Answer: Study of ferns

What is being done if they are *imbibing*?
Answer: They are drinking.

What does *deglutition* mean?
Answer: The act or process of swallowing

What is a *bellwort*?
Answer: A plant with yellow bell-shaped flowers

What is a *reichsmark*?
Answer: A monetary unit of Germany from 1925-1948

If a man brought an *ormolu* to his loved one, would he spend the night in the dog house or not?
Answer: Yes, it is an imitation of gold

The leader requests that all team members send their answer(s) via hardcopy or electronic versions at the end of the exercise.

Post-Work

Once the team building exercise has been completed, the next steps can be the following:

- The prizes can be sent out to the winning team members. (Prizes: Items can be as simple as an item for the work desk.)
- The leader can use a teaser and announce the next Virtual Team Building Exercise for the next team meeting.

Chapter 12 — Silent Auction

As familiar as people can get, an auction could inspire many team members to find out common interests. Requesting team members to submit items for auction can show common interests between various team members. One person's garbage could be another person's gold! Friendships have started on less common ground. Here is an interesting Virtual Team Building Exercise:

Pre-Work
- The leader can initiate the auction by requesting team members to offer items for auction that are of some value or that they feel display who they are and their interests.
- Items can be photographed and sent to the leader to share with the others prior to the auction start date
- The leader can provide the pictures via hardcopy, website (if possible), or one consolidated montage for viewing by all team members.
- The leader can determine the start and end date for the silent auction.

Playing the Virtual Team Building Exercise
- The leader can start the auction and let the team members know when it has begun and has ended (The best suggestion for the end date is the day before the next team meeting.)

- Each day during the auction, the daily bids are posted, and team members have a chance to outbid as the auction comes to a close.

Post-Work

Once the team building exercise has been completed, the next steps can be the following:

- The leader announces the final bids and the winners of the auctioned items.
- Photographs of the winners can be posted or sent via hard-copy in another montage.
- The items can be sent out to the winning team members.
- The money that was collected can be split with the team members that provided the item for auction, and the rest can be saved for a group get-together or for end-of-year acknowledgements of services and accomplishments that were completed during the year.
- The leader can use a teaser and announce the next Virtual Team Building Exercise for the next team meeting.

Final Thoughts

Based on many years of being part of team building exercises, virtual teams are commonplace in today's work environments. Trying to find ways to bond team members, using old styles in new ways, has shown that we all have common interests and enjoy a good time. Acknowledgement of one team member's achievements can enhance positive mental attitude amongst the entire team.

Should any of the Virtual Team Building Exercises listed within this book assist in enhancing team spirit, then we can assume it will spread to other teams. As team members move to other assignments or join other organizations, the feelings will continue. Memories and stories will be shared; thus, new ideas for Virtual Team Building Exercises can come to light.

Management support of this type of team interaction is essential to promote the positive mental attitude of all team members. Leaders can show that human resources (not just materials) are equally important and they must be maintained at a high level of respect. Team members can spend more time during their careers at work with team members than with their own families. Since so much time is spent together, why not build those relationships to increase a healthier work environment and possibly eliminate friction and unnecessary conflicts?

Thank you to everyone who has taken the time to understand the need for these types of interactive Virtual Team Building Exercises.